Finding Support in Ministry

Edited by

Nick Helm

Bishop of Sheffield's Chaplain and Advisor in Spirituality

and Philip Allin

Bishop of Sheffield's Advisor in Pastoral Care and Counselling

GROVE BOOKS LIMITED
RIDLEY HALL RD CAMBRIDGE CB3 9HU

Contents

The Authors

This booklet has been a group effort, and we are very grateful to the contributors for giving up their time and sharing their wisdom. We sought to cover some of the most significant areas of support currently around, and to draw upon a range of people from around the country to share their insights.

Audrey Attwood offers Spiritual Direction in South Yorkshire.

Gill Carding, Director of Counselling in the Diocese of Chester.

Andrew Walker, Rector of St Mary Woolnoth in the City of London and director of the London Centre for Spirituality.

David Tilley, CME Adviser in the Diocese of Coventry.

Michael Sadgrove, Dean of Sheffield Cathedral.

Phillip Tovey, Diocesan Training Officer in the Oxford Diocese.

Charles Chadwick, Vicar of Bridgwater St Mary, Chilton Trinity and Durleigh in the Diocese of Bath and Wells.

The Cover Illustration is by Peter Ashton

First Impression June 2002
ISSN 0144-171X
ISBN 1 85174 500 9

Nick Helm
Help...!

1

The unexamined life is not worth living.

Socrates

Ministry is a demanding calling to live out. Whether ministry is ordained or lay, it needs support, encouragement, and space for growth and learning from experience—both our own and other people's.

Finding ways of resourcing and supporting ministry can be difficult and challenging. I have been in ordained ministry now for over 14 years, and know well the confusion at various points through these years when I have felt that I had reached the limits of my personal resources. Was I expected simply to soldier on? Where could I turn to? What sort of support did I need? Would I be showing weakness that would be held against me in the future? What if the person I turned to did more harm than good?

For me some of these questions delayed my acting to find the support I needed. Having now experienced spiritual direction, psychotherapy, supervision, ministerial review and support groups I know that each in its own way has helped and enhanced my ministry. I know my ministry is the product of the generosity of spirit and support of God and of a number of key people. I no longer look at my ministry as something I exercise on my own—but know it to be supported by those who currently help me as well as those who have given me support in the past. I also know that without these sources of support I would probably have 'lost faith' and given up ministry ending up a cynical ex-minister.

I no longer look at my ministry as something I exercise on my own

This booklet is intended to help people in all forms of ministry to appreciate the variety of types of support available and to help them to decide which is most appropriate for them. Certainly my experience suggests that more than one will be necessary, and that over time some will become more important and others less so. We hope that this means that people will take up support sooner rather than later and rather than soldiering on develop a range of resources appropriate to the individual and to the demands of the ministry.

...I Need Somebody

Reflecting on one's life and actions cannot be an individual activity. We need the help of others to do this. There is a range of ways in which another person can help in this—from simply being a listener as we seek to look at ourselves honestly, to being someone who uses gifts, skills and experience to help explore, untangle, and recognize the nature of life and ministry. While my own experience provides a testimony of the value of supports, there are important theological, pastoral and personal reasons for seeking supports like those described here.

Theological

It is both the nature of God as Trinity and the nature of the ministry of Jesus in working with disciples that provide an understanding of mission and ministry that is mutual, supportive and relational.

The gospels, and particularly John's gospel, show Jesus revealing his need for support from those around him (not least in the garden of Gethsemane) and from his Father in prayer. The references to him taking or seeking time away from others for prayer show a pattern of spiritual resourcing. At his baptism and transfiguration Jesus' ministry is affirmed and confirmed by the Spirit coming down upon him. In the farewell discourses in John's gospel, we see a picture of mutual support in the Father who sends and the Son who was sent and was obedient to the mission of the Father. Thus the action of God the Trinity is revealed—the Father, who sent the Son, provides support through the sending, through the Spirit in moments of revelation and in the dynamic of prayer. There is a clear sense of supportive mutual mission, where each person of the Trinity plays a particular part.

Each person of the Trinity plays a particular part in a supportive mutual mission

Jesus' supportive fellowship with his disciples shows a ministry that is not exercised in isolation or independence of other people. At various times he checks out with them what they are making of him and his ministry. He also spends time with them giving them experiences of ministry, hearing their reports of what happened and providing his perspective on this. This enables both him to be aware of what is happening and the disciples to learn from their experience and reflect upon it.

Jesus' ministry was not exercised in isolation or independence other people

4

Pastoral

In ministry, particularly when it becomes stressful and overwhelming, we can find ourselves behaving in ways that we are surprised by, that feel uncharacteristic and undesired. Psychologically this may be our 'shadow' becoming manifest, though biblically it may be closer to Paul's description in Romans 7. 18–19: *'For I have the desire to do what is good, but I cannot carry it out. For what I do is not the good I want to do; no, the evil I do not want to do—this I keep on doing.'*

The history of the church is littered with examples of unredeemed attitudes

Equally there are always 'unredeemed' aspects of ourselves that prevent us from appreciating the nature of what we are faced with, and our attitudes and responses can lock us into unhelpful and unhealthy ways of ministry—unhelpful and unhealthy for those on the receiving end as well as those offering it. The history of the church is littered with examples of unredeemed attitudes leading to harmful pastoral effects, from the early church's attitude to gentiles and circumcision (redeemed in this case) to forms of ministerial abuse of power today.

Having good support and accountability within ministry is an essential aid to preventing some of the potential harm from occurring. It is not a guarantee, but it can help significantly.

Personal

Finally, there are very important personal reasons for seeking support. Ministry as a calling implies we are called as individuals and so ministry is an expression of oneself. Maintaining this integrity is not easy when there are powerful expectations around. These can be the expectations of others, or our own expectations of what we are seeking to be, which may be based not on who we are, but on some idealized projection of ourselves. To withstand this requires a spirituality that feeds our sense of personal identity and calling; we need places where it is supported and affirmed as well as explored, challenged and encouraged to develop.

Having support that recognizes us as individuals is far more likely to enable ministry with integrity than to be a self-indulgent waste of time. Again, there is no guarantee here, but as part of good and wise support this can be enormously helpful.

2

Audrey Attwood
Spiritual Direction

To be 'in spiritual direction' is not submitting to a person in authority over me who would give me 'directions' comparable to those he might give me if I asked advice on how to get from London to Leeds.

It is a relationship which has as its intention the enabling of the Holy Spirit's direction to be recognized and responded to by the person undergoing 'spiritual direction.' As such the term 'spiritual director' conjures up unhelpful and inaccurate images.

The relationship with my director would be more like asking a friend I trust to hold a torch so that I could see my own map more clearly and read it more accurately. The friend has some choice where it is directed and can offer some space to reflect on what is being seen and how to interpret the signs and symbols on the map.

In addition if I imagine that 'spiritual' means that I cannot talk about my everyday life but only about prayer, worship and my relationship with God then I would again be misunderstanding the practice of this ministry today. As William Barry points out, 'We must remember that in all aspects of his life the human being can only act as body-spirit, and any help towards personal development that overlooks this fact is likely to be more harmful than helpful to him.'[1]

What Happens in Spiritual Direction?

The focus of what I would wish to talk about in my visits to my director would indeed be my relationship with God and my journey with him, but very much as lived out in the reality of my everyday life, with all its joys and sorrows, blessings and struggles. Seeing the director as 'soul friend' conveys something important about the relationship so long as I did not infer from it that the sharing is two-way; my hour or hour and a half with my director would be *my* time and the agenda would be my own.

Another helpful title for director is 'spiritual companion.' It may help to highlight my sense of life as a journey during which I am growing and changing and choose to have someone I trust walk with me from time to time so that I can ponder out loud to her, air my concerns and be strengthened by what she may offer, in order to continue travelling with a little more sense of direction on my walk—what is helping it and what is getting in the way.

The interval between my visits to her might vary from monthly to three–monthly, though at the very beginning a few more frequent meetings may be suggested to establish the relationship and explore my 'story so far.'

What Makes Good Spiritual Direction?

a) Openness of the Directee

It will clearly be of much more benefit to my understanding of myself and where my life-giving energies come from if I am willing to try and be really open in my sharings with my director rather than deliberately wearing a mask in order to present a good or 'spiritual' front. This will involve taking my time to explore what I think and feel, what my reactions and responses were to the situation I want to talk about and also what might lie behind my unplanned reactions.

b) Attitude of Director

My director will not interrogate me! She will give me a safe space and ample time to open up at my own pace. She will be neither uncomfortable with my silences nor judgmental of what I say. She may help me to explore more deeply by asking occasional questions or offering pointers, for example:

- What was the effect of that on you?
- Where do you sense that was leading?
- Would you like to say a little more about that?
- Have you prayed about this? How?
- How is your prayer life going?
- How would you feel about trying praying in this way?

The Effect of Spiritual Direction

Ongoing spiritual direction will gradually help me to see the way more clearly, to discern the direction of my life and ministry. Although it will be especially welcome at times of uncertainty or possible change, it is not exclusively 'crisis management' so that I seek out a director only when in difficulties. The ongoing relationship of trust I have with my director, who gradually comes to know me well, will be a necessary basis which feels secure for me and also enables her to be alongside me in a more helpful way during times of confusion.

My experience of good spiritual direction will be that:

- I feel encouraged by it on my journey, occasionally challenged, always affirmed as a person and able to see more clearly where my own individual hindrances and helps are;
- I will be able to ask for suggestions for growing into a deeper prayer life and will gradually become more aware of my relationship with a loving God in both my prayer and my life;
- I will grow in faith, including through the darker times;
- I will gradually mature in my discernment and always have someone to help me test it. This might enable a greater boldness and a willingness to take risks.

Finding a Spiritual Director

The *National Retreat Association*[2] publishes a very useful leaflet entitled 'Choosing a spiritual guide.' It is helpful in encouraging the seeker, through a series of questions, to be clear about his or her requirements in a director.

In many dioceses there is usually an Advisor in Spirituality or similar who holds a list of local directors, and who can offer some suggestions in choosing a Spiritual Director or put you in touch with other counterparts.

It is worth considering people you have come across who may be able to provide spiritual companionship. Consider those who you have found spiritually encouraging, understanding, able to listen, people of spiritual depth.

> Prayer and spiritual direction are concerned with a relationship, not with magical solutions, and the relationship with the Lord, like any other relationship, is fostered and cherished because of the love of the other.

The good spiritual director will seek to mirror to you the unconditional love and acceptance of God.

> In the last analysis, (Christian) spiritual direction aims not at producing 'right choices'...or 'active apostles,' or 'clear-headed decision makers,' but at fostering a relationship, a relationship of Love. Those who are helped by spiritual direction will, we hope, work for the coming of the Kingdom of God on earth. We know many who do. But the spiritual direction they engage in has left them free to decide.[3]

Gill Carding
Counselling and Psychotherapy 3

Different people use the word counselling in different ways.

I use the term *therapeutic counselling* for what this chapter is about, in an attempt to distinguish it from active listening and the use of counselling skills as part of another role. I shall use the terms *therapeutic counselling* and *psychotherapy* interchangeably, but I shall say something about the nuances of these two names later in this chapter.

> Counselling is that activity which aims to help others towards *constructive change* in any or every aspect of life through a *caring relationship*, which has *agreed boundaries* and lays due emphasis on *psychological mechanisms*.[4]

Why and When to Seek Help

Pastoral ministry involves reaching out to people who are in distress and crisis. We are not offering effective caring if we are either untouched by the suffering of others or overwhelmed by it. We need to understand ourselves and to have faced and dealt with our own pain before we can fully engage with those who are in the throes of experiencing their pain.

Focusing on self can appear to run contrary to scriptural teaching about service and sacrifice. To admit that we are struggling psychologically and emotionally is taken as an indictment against the quality of our spiritual life; to acknowledge our human problems is somehow to deny the power of the Holy Spirit. I contend that in order to provide sustainable pastoral care, it is vital also to attend to self. With huge and conflicting expectations on those in ministry need to be firmly grounded in themselves as people, as well as in their Christian faith, if they are to withstand the pressures.

As human beings we are a wondrous mixture of inherited genes and diverse life experiences. Our constellation of life experience is as unique as our genetic blueprint, and it all has an impact upon shaping us into the person we become, with our own individual strengths and weaknesses. For some of us life and ministry play to our strengths for many years, and our vulnerabilities remain relatively unexposed. But we can all encounter situations where we discover that our usual ways of coping no longer work.

Common issues which may need to be addressed include past bereavements or losses which may have never been grieved. Our confidence and sense of worth is laid down in early childhood as a reaction to the response we receive from the adults around us. Where abuse or unremitting disapproval have been the stuff of daily existence, where lack of consistency and security have been an underlying feature, we may well carry into adulthood perceptions of ourselves which are unpleasant and inaccurate, as well as developing counterproductive behaviour patterns. It is quite possible for all this to co-exist alongside a conviction of God's love and acceptance. So it may be that we have learnt to appease the niggling doubts about ourselves by trying to please others and gain their approbation. This often shows itself in a problem with saying 'no.' But anyone in a leadership role who cannot say 'no' and take the consequences is likely to be heading for burnout or resentment amongst parishioners at lack of decision-making. Or we may feel that we are only good and worthwhile if we are constantly busy and doing for others. This tends to lead to problems in delegating, in letting go of responsibility and recognizing when we have done all we can. It also exacts a heavy price on our physical and mental health, and jeopardizes family relationships.

Therapeutic counselling involves exploring feelings, assumptions about self and others, and habitual ways of responding in order that a process of re-evaluation and change can take place.

Types of Therapeutic Counselling and Psychotherapy

The confusing array of therapies falls broadly into three categories:

- *Humanistic*, of which the most common is *person-centred*. This is a nondirective form of counselling which focuses upon present experiences and feelings as a means to uncovering past hurts and how these have undermined the confidence in the client's own perceptions and judgments. Although gentle, it can be challenging and thorough. It is particularly suitable for those who are constrained by many 'shoulds' and 'oughts,' and overly sensitive to the opinion of others.

- *Psychodynamic*. Here the emphasis is on gaining insight into unconscious processes, thereby providing the client with greater control and choice in their responses to people and situations. Attention will be given to early experiences and gradually connecting past events and feelings to current ones. Exploring the client's characteristic way of relating to others is a key element in the learning and growth. Psychodynamic counselling is appropriate for those who are troubled by confusing and conflicting feelings and reactions, and for whom understanding is important.

- *Cognitive-behavioural therapy (CBT)* concentrates on analysing thought and behaviour patterns. The sessions are more structured, with clearly defined goals. The client may sometimes be asked to do 'homework,' practising agreed tasks between sessions. CBT is proven to be effective with clients who are depressed or who tend towards a negative frame of mind. It is also beneficial in managing anxiety and overcoming a lack of assertiveness.

It is now generally recognized that no one type of therapy is intrinsically better than another. Rather, different models lend themselves to specific sorts of problem and person. There is increasingly a move towards counsellors and therapists being trained and practising in an integrative manner, offering flexibility in their approach to suit individual needs. Research has shown that the quality of relationship between *counsellor* and client is more important than the theoretical orientation of the *therapist*. Hence the crucial factor in choosing a therapist is to feel comfortable and at ease with him or her.

Returning to the issue of nomenclature, although there is no hard and fast rule regarding the distinction between the terms *counselling* and *psychotherapy* the following rough guidelines might be helpful. Counselling is more likely to be used for shorter, symptom-orientated work and psychotherapy for longer, deeper work. Those working from a person-centred approach are more likely to call themselves counsellors while those working within a psychodynamic framework tend to refer to themselves as psychotherapists.

Practicalities

- A therapeutic session will normally last an hour.

- Frequency is usually weekly, at least initially. Psychodynamic counselling may be more frequent at some stages in the therapy whereas CBT may be less frequent.

- The length of therapy varies enormously, from a single session to well over a year. An idea of timescale should be discussed in the initial session. Most counsellors will plan periodic reviews to take stock of progress and to check out that the client is getting what they need from the process.

- Therapeutic counselling and psychotherapy are not as yet statutory regulated occupations, so it is important to be discerning about the qualifications and expertise of any therapist you are considering seeing. The United Kingdom Council of Psychotherapists (UKCP) and The British Association for Counselling and Psychotherapy (BACP) are the main registering bodies. All members of these organizations adhere to the respective codes of ethics and good practice, and accredited or registered members will be fully qualified with a good deal of experience.

- Nearly all Anglican dioceses do have some arrangements for providing low cost or free therapeutic counselling/psychotherapy services and schemes exist for clergy in other denominations. However, these are not always well-publicised or readily accessible, and in the case of the Church of England the format differs considerably from diocese to diocese. Over half of GPs in England and Wales now offer counselling provision based in the surgery, although the number of sessions is often limited to six or eight. For all except perhaps those in the most remote areas there should be help at hand, but you may need to dig a little for it!

4

Andrew Walker

Supervision

Supervision is the providing of a space and some guidance to help us step back and rise above all we carry, to reflect with greater clarity from that changed and enhanced perspective.

It performs the same function as the traditional Christian practices of reviewing prayer and examining the day in the presence of God, but is focussed more specifically on our ministry and areas of effectiveness. It results in the same freedom that openness and humility before God always brings. The supervisor's role is ultimately to make him or herself redundant, facilitating the reflective process so that those being supervised come to engage with it for themselves.

But supervision can be understood in a number of different ways and not all are helpful to us in ministry. The core skills derive of course from contemporary society, where from the factory workshop to the psychotherapeutic couch supervision is a tool, often an invaluable one, for monitoring, evaluating and developing the skills and work of the one supervised. But when this model of supervision has been brought over wholesale into various diocesan schemes it can be seen as something imposed from outside or above. Issues of power are rarely clarified—Who is doing the supervising? Why? Where might the information go?—and some schemes have been introduced with little consultation, poor preparation or inadequate training. The resulting supervision can fatally combine more than one role—supervision, consultancy, mentoring, appraisal, and even spiritual direction. The minister can end up on the receiving end of a process that seems alien to the gospel and is actually counterproductive.

What of course we need to do is use many of the insights and experiences of the contemporary workplace, especially of those disciplines closest to our own, and interpret them in the light of Christian formation and as part of the process of modelling ourselves on the image of Jesus through the exercise of ministry today. Then we need to be clear what precisely we are about., clarifying for ourselves, as I will attempt to do below, the different tasks of supervision, the different needs of the supervisee, the different areas of possible focus. Then it can be free to become *our* supervision and not simply the opening up of our experience to the oversight of a visiting expert or authority figure.

The three areas mentioned above help define the role, function and usefulness of supervision, and we will look at them in turn.

The Tasks of Supervision

These fall into four main areas:

The Affirmative Task

Supervision must always be affirming and build up an individual's ministry. Note that this does not preclude the presence at times of challenge and confrontation, but the latter must always be made in love and with the desire to be constructive.

The Restorative Task

We all need places to 'let rip', be inappropriate, say things in a safe place where they will go no further. The 'toxic' material let out in this way is then off-loaded and no longer pollutes ministerial relationships and situations. Sometimes humour is all that is needed.

The Formative Task

By supervision we continue to cooperate in the process of being formed as disciples of Jesus and as apostles of the kingdom. This ongoing formation in the light of experience is crucial in integrating faith, life and ministry as God's revelation to us through everyday situations continues.

The Normative Task

There are norms of the workplace that we need reminding of, for example regarding professional or personal boundaries that can be under constant pressure. And there are values of the Kingdom which are countercultural and so may need conscious remembering. Supervision holds these for us and reminds us of them where appropriate.

The Supervisee's Developmental Stages

The level of experience of the supervisee will determine to an extent the level at which the supervision will be most effective and useful.

The Experience of Being a Novice

Whether as newly ordained, newly in a post or confronted by a new and unsettling situation (however experienced we may be in other areas), there will be times when we need high support to address the basic questions that sometimes arise. 'Am I in the right place?' 'Can I make it through this?' 'What do I need to do next?'

The Place of Apprenticeship

Once uncertainty and a natural degree of panic have died down, attention moves outwards and the areas of concern focus more on the external situation and the other people involved. Emotional support is still required, but so is reflection on skills and different possible approaches.

The Realm of the Colleague

The individual's training and learning here have been integrated much more into who we are, and so the reflection shifts onto the context or 'bigger picture' of the work and the situations brought. The supervision itself will be more collegial and will be hallmarked by sharing, exemplification and appropriate confrontation.

The Enjoyment of Wisdom

A mature place where the implications of all that is going on can be digested, current knowledge can be deepened, and our developing internal supervisor can be monitored and supported.

The Possible Points of Attention in Supervision

The supervisor or supervisee can choose to focus on any of the following:

- the internal experience of the supervisee ('I'm confused,' 'I suddenly feel fully confident');

- the relationship of the one supervised with work and ministry ('I am wondering what to focus on next,' 'My time off keeps getting eroded and I'm always tired');

- the specific skills and competencies used ('My use of bereavement visitors,' 'How I prepare for preaching');

- an individual or group situation confronting the one being supervised ('this group in the parish,' 'that PCC meeting');

- the norms of the workplace or kingdom values as they might apply ('How can I protect my home life?,' 'Remember the outcast');

- the internal experience of the supervisor can sometimes be relevant ('I notice I seem to be angry on my supervisee's behalf');

- the relationship between the supervisee and supervisor can be addressed ('We only ever seem/never seem to talk about areas of pain or failure. Why is that?').

Conclusion

Finding the right supervisor can be as important finding the right spiritual director and the relationship can be equally rewarding. Some dioceses have taken the trouble to train clergy as supervisors and we can turn to them as colleagues; others provide lists of lay people who work in this field. Some reflection will be needed on what aspect or aspects of supervision would be most attractive or useful for us, as this will facilitate the search. In all this the key factor is our formation in and through the ministry to which we have been called, and our ongoing response to the daily call of God to further integrate our life and work in the building of his kingdom.

5

David Tilley

Mentoring

Mentoring is an approach to personal and professional development in which an experienced colleague (mentor) acts as guide, adviser and supporter to a less experienced person (mentee).

The principal aim is to assist those being mentored to develop their expertise, so that ultimately they can stand on their own feet as capable people in a particular role or job. Mentoring is on-the-job learning and can provide support to a marginalized and pressured ministry and thus prevent burnout.

Mentoring focuses on the concerns and issues that arise in day-to-day practice

Mentoring focuses on the concerns and issues that arise in day-to-day practice and about which the mentee feels a need to consult. It is important that the mentor should not be the 'line manager,' since that person has a responsibility for the oversight and performance of the work. The mentor focuses on the mentee and his or her development. Thus issues about confidentiality need to be sorted out early in the relationship.

Why Mentoring? Why Now?

Recent developments in education and training have emphasized the importance of identifying individual learning goals and of work-based learning. We no longer assume that everybody needs to learn the same thing at the same time. This applies just as much to those in part-time or voluntary work, ordained and lay. The church now finds its ministry placed in a climate where reflective, creative and flexible leadership is required.

What Makes a Good Mentor?

People will bring their natural gifts and distinctive set of qualities into professional relationships. Nevertheless there are some broad but fundamental qualities desirable in mentors.

Professional Competence and Experience

Mentors need

- to be sufficiently out of their own initial learning in a job or role to have made the transition into self-managed ministry;
- to have a sufficient range of experience which parallels that expected in the work and role of the mentee;
- to identify and manage their own feelings about ministry;
- to feel secure and settled in their own role or profession.

They also need sufficient expertise in technical or legal matters, or knowledge about where to acquire it.

Good Interpersonal Skills

It is absolutely crucial that mentors have the ability

- to listen;
- to deal with differences of opinion;
- to ask open questions;
- to focus on the mentee's agenda;
- to use these skills for the benefit of the other person.

Commitment to Mentoring

Mentors need to be

- committed to the educational exercise and to take an interest in the personal and professional development of the mentee;
- confident about taking the initiative with the other person if the agreement is not to wane;
- sure only the best mentoring will do—and therefore accept responsibility for their own development.

Time and Accessibility

An effective mentor must be able to manage her or his own time so as to be available for regular meeting with the mentee. Availability in circumstances of crisis is necessary regardless of when the crisis occurs. The mentor is often the first person a mentee will turn to for help and advice.

Flexibility and Creativity

Mentors need to be flexible enough to tolerate and appreciate the uniqueness and individuality of the other person. It may happen that mentors will need to encourage development in areas he or she has not known or experienced. A mentor must be sufficiently confident in her or his own abilities not to be threatened by a different approach. It is just as important not to want to transform another person into a clone of oneself.

Spiritual Companionship

Mentoring is job- (or role-) related and is not spiritual guidance. Nevertheless, effective mentors in a religious context will value the wholeness of humanity and the wholeness of an individual. Clergy and ministers are people who see a close connection between who they are and what they do. Mentors will recognize the interrelation of the social, intellectual, emotional, psychological and spiritual sides of each person, and how dependent each is on the others for a whole ministry after the example of Christ.

Commitment to Monitoring and Evaluation

Mentors will be people who are willing

- to learn with other mentors;
- to celebrate success and mark good practice;
- to contribute their experience to a pool of knowledge that enables careful decisions to be made about mentoring in the church.

Ideas for a Mentoring Session

Review: how has the mentee followed up action or developments agreed at the last session? This is the only item that will not appear on the first occasion.

Concern: What is of concern to the mentee at present? Where is he or she feeling pressure?

Planning: What future work does the mentee want to think through or prepare?

Advice: What knowledge about technical, how-to-do-it, or legal issues concern the mentee? Where can they get more help?

Relational: Where in the mentee's work is conflict threatening? Where has it diminished?

Emotional and spiritual: How does the mentee feel about himself or herself at the moment? Is he getting time off? Coping with work and leisure boundaries? Enjoying both? What might the mentee want the mentor to remember in his or her prayers?

Issues for Agreement Between Mentor and Mentee

Essential Issues to be Agreed
- Where to meet—neutral territory or in a home?
- Frequency and duration of the sessions; monthly is desirable, six-weekly is probably the effective minimum.
- Confidentiality.
- Fees (if any) and expenses.
- Giving priority to the mentee's agenda—and whether items are to be notified in advance.
- Managing (or avoiding) interruptions.

Issues it is Desirable to Agree
- Accessibility to mentor outside sessions.
- Is note-taking useful and who will do it or will it be shared?
- When to review the arrangement and how it is working for both of you.
- Agreeing to meet even if there is no obvious agenda.

Issues that Might be Included
- Social elements, for example occasional lunches, whether partners are involved.
- Whether to pray or read the Bible together.

Ending the Mentoring Contract

When the time comes to end it is important the mentee feels he or she can take responsibility for the next phase. There may be an option to continue together for a finite period to conclude a piece of work. If you agree to end, a simple celebration or thanksgiving liturgy might be appropriate.

It is to be hoped that those who have been mentored effectively will see the value of it and want to train as a mentor themselves.

Finding a Mentor

Where do you look? The church's training and education advisers are obviously useful people to contact. Senior leaders such as archdeacons or district chairpersons could offer good advice. It is good to look for people who do not have another working relationship with you such as area or rural deans or spiritual guides. Many skilled people working in a secular environment would be willing to give time and skills to helping ministers in this way.

6

Michael Sadgrove

Ministerial Review

Ministerial review is increasingly practised in Anglican dioceses across the UK.

This welcome development follows the good practice of most secular organizations in requiring their employees to undertake regular appraisal. Appraisal systems vary largely from one organization to another, and not all of them are necessarily appropriate models for the church. (For instance, appraisal whose outcome may be performance-related pay adjustment will hardly apply to ordained ministers—at least, not yet.) For this reason, the term *ministerial review* suggests a broader and more comprehensive set of aims than *appraisal* or *assessment* and this is the term that I shall use in this section. I should also add that I am drawing mainly on the experience of ministerial review in the Diocese of Sheffield in which a review process for all stipendiary ordained and lay ministers has been in place for a decade.

Why Ministerial Review?

- It gives expression to the accountability of ministers to the bishop and the whole church.

- It is a sign of the pastoral care and concern for ministers by the bishop and by the church.

- It is a tool that enables ministers to reflect on their present work, learn from the past and set objectives for the future.

The Practice of Ministerial Review

a) Who Conducts Ministerial Review?

There is a wide variety of practice, from near '360 degree review' through peer review to the more traditional hierarchical process. Different systems fulfil different needs; informal patterns may well run alongside more formal ones and offer additional, more frequent, sources of support.

b) Frequency of Ministerial Review

Ideally, this should happen every year. This will not always be practicable. The minimum, if review is to be effective, is probably every other year, with a briefer follow-up meeting to check on progress at the half-way stage.

c) Preparation

Review needs preparation on the part of both minister and reviewer. A *pro forma* questionnaire is very helpful and needs to cover:

- what the minister understands to be the nature of the task;
- progress since the last review, including objectives set then, and how they have been met;
- particular issues currently being faced;
- what he or she regards as key strengths and weaknesses;
- where training or development is needed;
- objectives for the period up to the next review;
- longer-term hopes and aspirations;
- matters the minister wishes to bring to the attention of the bishop or diocese;
- family or personal matters the minister wishes to raise.

This is best provided to the reviewer in advance of the meeting to allow for reflection and preparation for the meeting.

d) The Interview

This should be conducted in a safe uninterrupted space with an agreement about the length of time to be given. Expect to spend between one and a half and two hours.

The agenda for the meeting is that set out by the minister in the completed questionnaire. The reviewer *must* take careful notes of the meeting, since a report will need to written up subsequently.

It is important to be focused on the task of review, which is *ministry- and work-related*. While a minister may wish to explore personal or family matters with the reviewer, this is not the occasion for in-depth pastoral support, spiritual direction, counselling or psychotherapy. Clearly, where more intensive pastoral support is needed, identifying how and where it is to be obtained is an important and legitimate task. Good empathetic listening is importantly the major tool of the reviewer.

Actions for the future should be agreed and highlighted. These may be for both reviewee and reviewer.

The minister should be reassured that the content of the conversation is confidential to the two of them. The report arising out of the meeting has a slightly different status (see the next section).

e) Follow Up

The reviewer writes up the interview as soon as possible, while the material is still fresh. The report should then be sent to the minister so that he or she can agree it and countersign it. If there are aspects of it with which the minister disagrees these are negotiated before a final text is signed off. If the reviewer and minister cannot agree, the minister is permitted to add his or her note of dissent in writing. This document is then sent to the bishop with a copy remaining with the minister for reference and action. Interim follow-up meetings on a six-monthly or annual basis can help keep the targets of review in focus, and convey the message that the institution continues to care about the welfare of its ministers and is committed to enabling them to reach their potential.

f) Confidentiality

Where ministerial review is, as has been described here, an episcopal and ecclesial function on this model of review, the confidentiality of the report is held not by the reviewer or bishop individually, but by the church as the institution responsible for the public conduct of its ministers. This means that like any other report or reference, it remains on the minister's personal file, and may in principle be consulted by those with a clear right to access privileged information. (This includes, under the Data Protection Act, the minister him- or herself.) Hence the importance of ensuring that the report gives a scrupulously fair (and agreed) account of the ministerial review.

Conclusion

While ministerial review can often be feared to be the hard face of the institution, creating anxiety and fear of weakness being exposed, its practice and the experience of many is that it is helpful, supportive and that weaknesses exposed are cared for and helped rather than judged as failures.

It is possible, where ministerial review is not part of the structure of the church or diocese, to instigate it for oneself, even to the point of having a report sent to the bishop or equivalent. It is worth looking for someone who has both significant ministerial experience and who has some insight into ways in which ministry can be helpfully reviewed and developed. Asking someone to do it, getting hold of sample questionnaires and agreeing a process, bearing in mind some of the points made in this chapter, is not going to be too onerous a task and may well pay dividends.

Nick Helm
Support Groups

7

Support group, cell group, peer group, reference group, supervision group...

Many different types of groups can provide support vital to ministry. Here I wish to focus on two types of group that seek to provide personal support.

- *Peer group* or *Cell group:* Here all members are likely to be peers having trained together, or worked in an area together and come together to share as equals and in so doing give and receive mutual support and encouragement.
- *Support group:* This is gathered to support one person in his or her ministry. The group members will have different lengths and levels of experience, and may have particular areas of expertise.

Establishing a Group

In establishing a group it is important to have clarity about its purpose, focus and way of working. The following points are worth considering prior to inviting people onto the group, or for peer groups as part of the process of exploring the possibilities of setting one up.

Purpose and Focus

- Is this group for providing mutual support or support for one person or somewhere between? If somewhere between, can you clarify how far along the spectrum you want it to be?
- Will the focus of attention be only on the person's work, or their work with some attention on its impact on other aspects of life and responsibilities, or covering all of their life?

Boundaries

What are the boundaries of the group—particularly on confidentiality? All too often it is found that 'confidentiality' is defined as 'telling just one person at a time' rather than not divulging anything that another member of the group has shared to anyone outside the group.

Ways of Working

- How often will the group meet and for how long?
- What level of commitment is asked of members?
- How will the meeting happen? For example, timetable, agenda setting, calling meetings, facilitating the process...
- What sort of response to contributions will be appropriate? The nature of the response can have a significant impact on how helpful this time is. Some ways are silent honouring of a contribution without verbal response, personal response (affirmation, sympathy etc), suggestions, asking questions, probing, challenging, prayer ministry, prayer support. Watch out for hijackers! ('that reminds me...')
- What is the long-term expectation of the group? Is it expected to last for decades (as a peer group may) or a few years (for the duration of a particular post)?
- Will the group have a process of reviewing itself? Will it set aside time to reflect on how it is going, what expectations are being met and which are not being met? How often should this be done?

Size and Membership

The size and makeup of the group will have a significant effect on how it works and how effective it becomes. Groups can range from about four to about a dozen. The level of trust and support needed and the nature and purpose of the group will have a bearing here. A small group can provide an opportunity for deep personal sharing and support, but may not offer much range of perspective.

The membership of a support group can be crucial. It is worth giving a good amount of time to pray and reflect about who is most appropriate to invite.

For a support group consider those

- currently involved in the area of ministry
- operating in related areas of ministry
- 'friends' of your ministry
- from different denominations
- from geographical areas further away

Getting Going

Consider what will help build up trust and support in the group. Would an external 'facilitator' help?

In the early stages of a group, and again at times when new members join, it is important to spend time discussing the principles and process, talking them through so that there is clarity, and to ensure the discussion relates to them. Often this can feel less productive, and away from the prime focus, but where this is done well the effect on the way the group performs will be noticeable.

Classic group theory suggests that groups go through the stages of forming, storming, norming and performing. A fifth stage of re-forming will also happen from time to time. These processes will inevitably occur as part of a support group and it is important to recognize, accept and appreciate the benefit of working through these stages. Holding an awareness of the foundational principles of the group, its intention and purpose, and the commitment of the members to the group will help a group to work through the more difficult stages of this process.

Value of Group

The effect of a support group can be very valuable and significant. It is likely to include:

- a sense of support
- reduced feelings of isolation
- the discipline of stopping and reflecting
- the benefit of learning from others

Groups can have great synergy, but also can be great drains. Watch what yours is doing.

Setting One Up

In setting support groups up, there is no hard and fast principle. The initiative can be taken at any time. It then becomes a matter of doing the homework and the donkey work. The homework is to clarify the nature, purpose and intention of the group and thinking through some of the points raised above. The donkey work is to talk to people, gather the group, and then talk through and clarify as a group what it is all about.

Key to setting up a group is the matter of setting aside time and space to do it. Keep coming back to any sense of vision you have for it. This will help you find the energy to plan and act. Once it is established, the challenge of trusting and letting support grow will be faced in both obvious and subtle ways. It is important to review the group from time to time, and where necessary changing or ending the group.

8

Phillip Tovey and Charles Chadwick
Learning Partnerships

Learning partnerships are used in education particularly in part-time or distance learning programmes.

One of the problems here is isolation. If students meet up to discuss the course outside of formal classes, then it has been shown that this helps foster learning. The characteristics of a learning partnership are:

- a structured, but informal opportunity for people to learn together;
- a means of learning new approaches to issues from another person's observations;
- learning takes place in an experiential context;
- non-judgmental and positive;
- fosters learning by reflection;
- enhances listening skills.

Why Did We Get Involved?

For one year we participated together in a learning partnership. We had known one another for many years being in the same CME group and then meeting up for lunch to discuss how things were going. We both got involved in experiential learning courses and this led to us organizing ourselves into a more formalized support and developmental approach. This ended when Charles changed job and moved to another diocese.

We came across the work of the Ontario Institute for Adult Education, which seemed to us to have relevance for parish ministry.[4] We were interested in questions like: how can ministers find support? How can we develop in our ministry? How do we learn from other ministers, when much of what we do is alone?

How do we learn from other ministers when much of what we do is alone?

How We Set It Up

Our learning partnership was set up in this way:

- We contracted to meet once a month for 2 hours. This was based around lunch (mostly in a pub).
- The format was for one person to bring a piece of ministry and speak about the learning that was going on. The other listened, asking questions for clarification and gradually asking more probing questions. The aim in this phase was not to provide answers but to gently dig into what was going on.
- This process was then reversed with the other person leading.
- We also kept journals in part to capture events to talk about but also to look at the partnership itself and what we thought was happening.
- At the end of a year we had a review of the meetings.

This was a format that we found worked even with both of us having busy ministries.

We found that time pressures were great and that day-to-day commitments like funerals meant that we had to defend the time. In part this was saved by a firm contract at the outset, that we would stick to the meetings and make them a priority. Sometimes we renegotiated the time but we adhered to a monthly meeting. We also found that it worked better when the focus was a live issu—one to which there is some emotional attachment about what is going on. This was not the same as talking about a book that was being read.

What is Distinctive about a Learning Partnership?

There are a number of features that make the learning partnership different.

- It is outside the formal structures of the diocese.
- It is not appraisal, done with hierarchs or specialists.
- It is not work consultancy, done with a trained consultant.
- It is not spiritual direction, as it concentrates more on work.

So Why Did It Work for Us?

- Part of the success was the fact that it was based on friendship, two clergy supporting one another.
- It was confidential—nothing was to go outside the pairing and there was nobody to report to.

This mutuality is one of the features of the learning partnership that is its strength. It also means that it is easy to set it up without involving 'officials.'

We also found that the nature of the partnership was such that we learned a lot about one another and our friendship flourished. We learned things about one another in a supportive way, not coloured by competition that clergy can get into. Clearly boundaries are important here. It was easy to let the pastoral issues come to the fore after a while and we had to remind ourselves of the aim—learning about ministry. It was not a therapy session, but clearly our feelings colour our actions in ministry.

What Difference did this Make?

We were quite committed to following a Kolbian learning cycle. This approach works from a concrete experience by examining that experience, reflecting on it to discover the learning, and then planning some action, which in turn becomes the next experience. So often we would plan some action at the meeting and bring this back to the next meeting. We found that the mutual support was key for bits of ministry that were tough. Often gifts and insights could be used to look at some work in a different way.

It has become something that we have recommended to others in training. We have also gone on to develop it in different ways in our new ministries.

How Might You Set Up a Learning Partnership?

If you want to set up such a partnership you should consider:

- The contract you are going to make: With whom are you going to meet? How often? For how long each session? For how many sessions? What are you going to do?
- Building in review for each session and a set of sessions.
- The place you might give to keeping a journal in the partnership.
- How you are going to approach a partner.

Once a partnership is set up you might consider:

- How you are benefiting.
- The lifecycle of the partnership.
- When to end.

Philip Allin

The End Game or Knock, Ask, Seek

9

Reflective Practitioners?

How may we become 'reflective practitioners' in the art of ministry? This is of course a lifetime's labour of love, and pivotal to vocation. It is surprising, though, how quickly it becomes relegated to the 'outhouse' of our life and work! This relegation (or is it denial?) is always done for the very best of all possible motives—the demands of the gospel are great; mission and evangelism are, rightly, given a priority; pastoral care is an urgent necessity and then there is the administration…

Ministers are caring people. However, in truth we are often drawn to care for others by a host of motivations and quite honestly it is simpler caring for others than for ourselves or those closest to us. The many demands of ministry give ample opportunity to avoid responsibilities closer to home.

Detachment and Attachment

These are technical terms from both the Christian spiritual tradition and the world of psychotherapy, and alert us to a real danger for ministers—lay and ordained. Spirituality urges detachment as an essential quality in the quest to deepen relationship with God—to detach from those things that get in the way of this most central of all relationships. Ministry may be a sign of such detachment when a person's primary focus becomes a desire to deepen this relationship—by a grappling with those things that divert from the task. But there is a paradox here. Effective ministry demands attachment, not only in a spiritual/theological sense, but in a psychological one as well. Ministry without attachment can be experienced as cold, withdrawn, distant, even critical, whereas attachment without the balance of detachment may become overwhelming, restricting and depersonalizing. One of the many tasks in ministry is to hold these two tensions in a creative and liberating way for the individual. I write 'one of the many' but it is probably the most important skill to learn and hone in the practice of ministry. Living in paradox, in the creative balance, holding the tension with others, proclaiming truth in an unheeding world are the causes of extreme pressure and thus stress for those in ministry. Issues of detachment and attachment are at the heart of this creative process.

Support in Paradox

Where may the minister discover the necessary support and encouragement to engage with this task? In seeking meaning for others in Christ, how may they be affirmed in their own faith journey and develop an appropriate sense of maturity for themselves in relation to God, the institution of the church and the local *ecclesia*? The answer lies in the tried and trusted pathways of the Christian tradition:

- Reflective study
- Companionship
- Readiness to be vulnerable
- Reality of spiritual journey
- Prayer—especially that of inner stillness

In these the support, insight, and wisdom of an other is crucial. Ministry without this is often open to considerable damage to the minister and to others. This booklet has sought to open the possibilities of networks engaging with the sensitive task of monitoring, supporting, reviewing—all within the context of spiritual friendship. The contributions are by experienced and committed practitioners and offer the potential to engage in the individuation process—the deepening of relationship with God, with self and with others.

Metaphors of Hope

Not for a long time has the Christian's search for God been so full of movement. The metaphor of *journey* is central to the faith of many and pilgrimage is a specific outward expression of the journey which for many of us is an inward one, a journey to the soul's core where the living God is to be known.

In this journey new faith is confirmed and old faith is renewed—both are transformed. Most often, like the Canterbury pilgrims of old, there is a corporate edge to an intensely spiritual experience. People encourage and affirm one another and in this activity there seems to be an intense listening—to God, to other, to self. This movement of the Holy Spirit can be known in many Christian communities—there is a deep desire to mature and deepen personal faith which in turn can be threatening to the local minister, particularly if he or she has not become a part of the momentum! A spiritual, seeking church will need ministers with depth, insight and sensitivity, leaders in the mould of and in the stature of Jesus Christ. Metaphors are important concepts—take care they do become realities. With that comes responsibility.

Help—I Need Somebody!

How are ministers and priests to find the appropriate help they need? Before tackling the question I want to speak personally. I have been in ministry for over 30 years and have come to realize just how valuable for my work and being are the approaches outlined in this book—now—but it was not always thus. The realization that I needed help was slow to dawn. There was a self sufficiency in this that bordered on arrogance. I spent the first 12 or so years of ministry flailing around without focus or guidance, constantly expecting the church leadership to give what in fact it was not able to give— they had become my idealized parent figures. One bishop had said 'I am your Father in God, but I am also your employer.'

Life became less complicated and I became more at ease when I began to take responsibility for my own life and actions—trusting God. Here, in part, lies the answer to the question 'How can I get the support necessary for me to minister effectively?' Go out and find it for yourself. Make explorations. Remember that the choice of today may not be appropriate in 5 years time.

In the strength of the church is its weakness. A firm structure is important, but when the structure is pyramidal and is parental, patriarchal indeed, the chances are that it will elicit a dependent, childish response from those who look to it for nurture. The minister's attachment to the institution is a real problem—how to positively separate and become an adult? This dynamic will include loss and its attendant grief and anger—but in the end will be gain for minister and church. For the loyal servant of the church this will seem frightening and yet not to tread this path is to remain in thrall to our immature needs. The movement is from bondage to freedom—a principle supported by our theology and tradition.

Go out and find out for yourself. Be bold! Adventure! Taste and see!

The role of the minister within the church has to be that of a mature adult—aware of being, at appropriate times, parent to the 'flock,' but also being aware of the 'inner child' and its needs for nurture. Maturity does not deny the integral parts of ourselves, but loves, cherishes and unifies into that place where our dependency should be—in Jesus Christ.

How Do They Do That?

How do we do that—how do we take on the full stature of Christ? Where can we look for help? First act on what you have read here. Be bold! Adventure! Taste and see! The minister who takes responsibility for self in the vulnerability of ministry has embarked on the path that leads to being a mature reflecting practitioner.

The End Game is a movement towards that wholeness of body, mind and spirit which is irresistibly attractive in Jesus, in whom we are called to live, grow and have our being.

Bibliography

Spiritual Direction

K Leech, *Soul Friend—Spiritual Direction in the Modern World* (DLT, 1994)
M Geunther, *Holy Listening—The Art of Spiritual Direction* (DLT, 1992)
E Peterson, *Working the Angles—the Shape of Pastoral Integrity* (Eerdmans, 1997)
A Long, *Approaches to Spiritual Direction* (Grove Spirituality booklet S 9)

Counselling and Psychotherapy

R Hurding, *Roots and Shoots* (Hodder, 1986)
M Jacobs, *Still Small Voice* (SPCK, 1990)

Supervision, Mentoring and Groups

J Foskett and D Lyall, *Helping the Helpers: Supervision and Pastoral Care* (SPCK, 1994)
P Hawkins, *Supervision in the Helping Professions* (OUP, 2001)
J Mallinson, *Mentoring to Make Disciples and Leaders* (Scripture Union, 1999)
L M English, *Mentoring In Religious Education* (Religious Education Press)
E Parsloe, *The Manager As Coach And Mentor* (Institute of Personnel and Development 1999)
C Chadwick and P Tovey, *Growing In Ministry: Using Critical incident Analysis* (Grove Pastoral booklet P 84)
C Widdicombe, *Group Meetings that Work: A Practical Guide for Working with Different Kinds of Groups* (St Paul's, 1994)

Finding Support

D Heard and B Lake, *The Challenge of Attachment for Caregiving* (Routledge, 1997)
J Holmes, *John Bowlby and Attachment Theory* (Routledge, 1993)
C Edmondson, *Minister Love Thyself!* (Grove Pastoral booklet P 83)

Notes

1   William A Barry and William J Connolly, *The Practice of Spiritual Direction* (HarperCollins).
2   Both quotations here are from Barry and Connolly.
3   National Retreat Association, Central Hall, 256 Bermondsey Rd, London SE1 3UJ.
4   Hurding, R, *The Bible and Counselling* (Hodder & Stoughton, 1992). A succinct account of distinctions between spiritual direction, therapeutic counselling and healing.
5   Robinson, J, Saberton, S and Griffin, V, *Learning Partnerships: Interdependent Learning in Adult Education,* (Ontario: Ontario Institute of Adult Education, 1985).
6   See Matthew 10.37–38, Colossians 3.9–10, Ephesians 4.22–24.